HAUNTED INNS

Enjoy!
Kathi MacIver

By
Kathi Mac Iver

HAUNTED INNS

Kathi Mac Iver

Published by:
Columbine Press
PO Box 1950
Cripple Creek, CO 80813

First printing 1998

ISBN 0-9651272-5-7

Printed in the United States of America

Introduction

Ghosts are creepy, hair-raising and terrifying. Or are they?

Ghosts come in many forms. Professor Hans Holzer tells us in his book entitled, "Ghosts", that all humans have a physical body and an etheric body also known as soul, psyche or personality. At death, the two separate, the physical body quickly decaying; the soul going its own way. *Where* it goes depends on one's personal religious beliefs.

Sometimes, when death comes suddenly and violently, the soul of the deceased is confused. It is incapable of moving on. It often continues the daily activities to which it was accustomed when the body was alive. Such a lost soul, according to Holzer, is known as a ghost. A true ghost is unaware of living persons, of the passing of time, indeed of its own death.

Eddie, in the Victor Hotel, is a ghost.

A free spirit, on the other hand, is quite content with its earthly abode and chooses not to leave. It is very much aware of living persons and attempts to make contact with them. It may make noises or movements to attract attention, may allow itself to be seen, may even speak.

Such is the perpetual host of the Last Dollar Inn.

A small and mischievous free spirit is known as a hobgoblin, writes Rosemary Ellen Guiley in her book, "The Encyclopedia of Ghosts and Spirits." This description fits little Petey of the Hotel St. Nicholas. Petey was probably one of the many orphans cared for at the old St. Nicholas Hospital. The loving nuns were his family. The laundry room where he did his chores may be the only home he remembers. So he has adopted the present occupants, playing pranks to make himself known.

Why are such phantoms so prevalent in the Cripple Creek District? That question has yet to be answered.

The Last Dollar Inn
And
Humorous Parking Sign

LAST DOLLAR INN

A crooked little house
On a crooked little street
In a crooked little town
Called Cripple Creek.

After Janice and Rick Wood moved into the house at 315 East Carr, they found this little poem among papers left in the house by a previous owner.

They laughed and told each other that is exactly what it is, and they love it that way.

Buying the hundred-year-old house, restoring it and adding an addition was a tremendous job. Rick and his father, Don, did most of the work. Janice and Rick's mother, Jean, painted and wallpapered. Then they added carpets, curtains and drapes, antique furniture, fluffy bedspreads, and Victorian accessories. The result is one of the loveliest Bed and Breakfast Inns in the Pikes Peak area. Janice makes guests as comfy as possible. Rick tells ghost stories and cooks a gourmet breakfast.

The Woods are former residents of Colorado Springs and have loved Cripple Creek for years. Living here is a long sought dream. In choosing the "crooked little house,"

3

they bought more than they bargained for. Just before signing the escrow papers, their realtor informed them they were purchasing what may be the most haunted house in Cripple Creek. Janice was skeptical, but Rick was delighted. A successful Cripple Creek inn needed ghosts!

I interviewed Janice and Rick in the old house, the bricks faded almost pink in one hundred years. In the front window, a stained glass rendition of St. Francis welcomed me as it has always beckoned to everyone driving by. The parlor glowed in the mid-day sun. The décor, furnishings and knick-knacks made me think the wrong calendar hung on the wall. It must surely be 1898, not 1998. I thought about the people to whom that house had been home. People whose lives were ordinary and extra-ordinary, for 315 East Carr has been the address for several multi-talented folks.

Janice began our interview by telling me of her feeling about ghosts and spirits.

Janice: I can't really believe in ghosts. I guess I want something to manifest itself. I have to reach out and touch something to believe it is really there. There are certain feelings here, like a warm, caring spirit, perhaps. There are noises, even shadows, sometimes. But are they ghosts?

Rick: Of course there are ghosts here. There is no other way to explain it. And they are welcome. After all, they have welcomed us.

Kathi: Have you ever been frightened?

Rick: Only once. I was scared to pieces. I walked past that picture, there, and saw Janice's face, reflected in the glass. She had gone into Colorado Springs and wasn't due back for several hours. Seeing her face made me think something was wrong. An accident, maybe. Those hours of waiting until she drove up were the longest of my life.

Kathi: You thought the spirits were sending you a message regarding your wife?

Rick: Of course. What else could it be? I've no idea what message, since Janice had not had any trouble. But it made me realize there is a positive power in this house – the power of the dead but not departed.

Janice: He's so sure. I wish I could be.

Rick: Yes, I'm sure. How could I not be certain when I am called by name?

Kathi: A ghost knew your name? And spoke it?

Rick: Yes. I get up early to prepare breakfast. I was puttering around one morning, all by myself, when someone at my shoulder said, "Hello, Rick!"

Kathi: How did you feel? Frightened?

Rick: No! I was excited! I wanted to turn around and shake hands. I wanted to know what he looked like. I wanted to sit down and talk with him. I had wondered about him for so long. I still don't know his name, but he knows mine. I am thrilled about it.

Kathi: Is he the only ghost in the house?

Rick: There is a lot of activity in this house. But, yes, I think he is the only one who resides here. And, I believe he does reside here, just as he did years ago. He has guests, one or two at a time. He has parties, as well, with a lot of people. Those other people have been heard, talking, laughing, and even dancing. But I think only one man lives here. It is his home and he wants us to know that we are his guests, as well.

Kathi: He seems to have taken a liking to you.

Rick: He has. We would have been great friends had

Saint Francis of Assisi
Stained-glass window

	we lived in the same era.
Kathi:	You have not felt this closeness, Janice?
Janice:	No, not at all. Perhaps because he is a man.
Kathi:	Tell me again the story of your first night here.
Janice:	It was Halloween. We were sleeping on the floor, here in the parlor. I was so tired. I was in a lot of pain from my back. I'd had back trouble for eight years. I wondered if sleeping on the floor was a terrible mistake. I couldn't go to sleep. I turned and tossed and mentally added chores to my list of "things to do tomorrow." It seemed there was simply not enough time or energy to get everything done.

The light from the street came through the stained-glass window, leaving colored spots everywhere. I didn't know who the man depicted in the window was supposed to be, but I assumed it was a Biblical character. The words above his head are "Expect a miracle." I kept thinking, it will be a miracle if I get through this night. But I kept my eyes on the window, reading over and over, "Expect a miracle." Finally, I went to sleep.

In the morning I woke up feeling more rested than I had for months. During the day I told Rick I felt so good. My back did not hurt one bit! More than that, it has not hurt since! That was my miracle.

| Kathi: | Your back troubled you for eight years, but has not given you any pain since that first night here? |
| Janice: | Isn't that amazing? Later someone told me that the man in the window is St. Francis, who loved animals and birds. He healed them and cared for them. I can't say if that has anything to do with my back. But, something happened. |

7

Antique Lamp

Kathi: A miracle?

Janice: I guess. It must have been.

Kathi: What else has left you wondering.

Janice: Little things. See this lamp here. It's a typical Victorian style with a painted glass globe. This one has crystals hanging down around the globe. You have to reach through the crystals to turn the lamp on and off. I do that every night. Of course the crystals hit each other as you touch them, making a tinkling sound. One night I turned it on and then walked toward the dining room. The crystals began to tinkle again. I watched the crystals sway and heard that sound. Then they stopped.

Kathi: Did you think a ghost touched the lamp?

Janice: No. I thought the crystals had gotten caught in each other, then one fell in place and started them all tinkling.

Kathi: Still, you wonder...

Janice: Yes. I must admit, I do.

Kathi: What else has left you wondering?

Janice: Well, there was this shadow...

Rick: She calls it a shadow, but it was not a shadow. A shadow is on the ground, right? This was a black spot, about the size of a football or maybe a little bigger that moved across the archway into the dining room, about a foot off the ground.

Janice: There were some other people here.

Rick: Yes, a couple with a baby. The baby had been really fussy, crying so we could hardly hear each other talk. The mother got up to walk, bouncing the baby up and down and crooning to her. I saw this black spot at the right of the door. I looked at Janice. She sat up straight, her eyes big as saucers. I knew she saw it, too.

Parlor and Dining Room

Janice: I thought it was a shadow of something moving outside the house.

Rick: But nothing was out there. And there were no lights there so there could not have been a shadow. You asked, Is someone there? Remember? So you knew it was more than a shadow, even if you won't let yourself believe it. Anyway the mother was there in the archway and I watched that spot move to the left, slowly. The mother was watching it, too. The spot moved between the woman and me! I saw it pass in front of her. Then all of a sudden the baby stopped crying and was as good as she could be.

Kathi: So you think this spot, whatever or whoever it was, calmed a crying baby?

Rick: It did.

Kathi: And three of you saw it?

Rick: Yes. The man was sitting with his back to the doorway and was looking at the stained glass window. He didn't see it, but he turned around and asked, "What's going on?"

Janice: I asked the woman, later, what she thought about it. She said she didn't even remember it. That she didn't believe in ghosts or things like that.

Kathi: And you still think it was only a shadow?

Janice: I don't know.

Rick: Sometimes when people first walk in, they talk about a man standing in that corner.

Kathi: Have you seen a man in the corner?

Rick: No.

Janice: No. But, several people have mentioned it. Of course no one is there. One man swore up and down that it was Tesla.

Kathi: Tesla?

11

Two Bedrooms in the Last Dollar Inn

Janice: Yes, Nikola Tesla. Have you heard of him?

Kathi: Yes.   Vaguely.   He was an inventor or something?

Rick: Actually he was an electrical engineer. He did a lot of things with electricity that no one else had tried. He was before his time and a lot of people thought he was crazy. Of course people are quick to think anyone is a nut, just because they might be smarter. Among other things, Tesla demonstrated how a magnetic field could be made to rotate by supplying two coils at right angles with alternating current. Which led to his patenting the alternating-current motor.

Janice: What was that thing in the front yard?

Rick: One man claimed he had seen a vortex in the front yard. You know, a whirlwind. Tesla often referred to the action of a vortex. He said a vortex was a mass of fire, air or water rotating rapidly around an axis and that helped explain some of his experiments.

          I asked several old timers if they thought Tesla was in Cripple Creek at one time. Of course, he traveled all over. But it's not surprising that he might have been here. We know he was in Colorado Springs for a time. The mines in this area were known worldwide for their innovative sources of power. Tesla would have wanted to know all about that. He may even have given them some ideas.

Kathi: When might this have been?

Rick: He died in 1943, I think. He was an old man, then. So I suppose it was maybe the '20's? I went down to the Tesla museum in Colorado Springs. Sure learned a lot of things that we didn't learn in school. Apparently Tesla did

	visit Cripple Creek, but I couldn't verify he was ever in this particular house.
Janice:	Yet, a number or people have claimed they saw Tesla standing in the corner of my living room!
Kathi:	They may have been right. On the other hand, perhaps it is your permanent host; the man who still lives here and welcomes all your guests, as well as his?
Rick:	That sounds more likely. Personally, I would like Tesla to come back. Wouldn't that be something?
Kathi:	Tell me some of your other guests' experiences.
Rick:	We had a guest ask how far away the train station was. This was in the wintertime and our little tourist train was not running. I told her I guessed the closest station was Canyon City. She said she was sure she heard a train in the night.
Janice:	Another man asked how many trains there were. He said he heard train whistles all night long. I told him in the past, there were fifty trains every day in and out of Cripple Creek. He said he had heard them all!
Rick:	One woman said someone walked up and down the hall past her door. I explained to her that her door was at the end of the hall. Someone might have walked up to her door, but they couldn't walk past it unless they walked through a wall.
Janice:	And then there was the doorbell.
Rick:	This has gotten to be the most popular story. One morning a woman stood out in the yard. I invited her in, but she would not come in. She said she was the daughter of the last owner, who had recently died. The daughter had come

to clear out the house, soon after her mother's death. But she said she simply could not cope with the situation. She fled the house, leaving her mothers papers and other things behind.

Kathi: What upset her so?

Rick: The doorbell ringing. She would go to the door again and again, but no one was there. Then she stood at the window and later around the corner of the house to catch whoever was annoying her by ringing the bell and running away. She never found anyone. I led her up to the porch and pointed out that there was no doorbell. She turned very pale. I told her that when we replaced the molding around the door, we found the bell button underneath the molding! We, too, had heard this story of the doorbell ringing, and were as shocked as she when we found the button. I traced the wiring and found it had been burned out for several feet. There was no way the bell could have rung, even if someone had found the button to push. The daughter went away. I don't know if she felt better or worse.

Janice: This woman who lived here, years before we came along, was very well known. She died just before we moved in. She did not die in this house; she was ill and in a nursing home. But people brought flowers and left them on our step. There were dozens of bouquets and they kept coming for weeks. I took a picture. After it was developed I saw there was a cat sitting on the step beside all the flowers. The neighbors had called her the cat lady because she liked cats and had a dozen or more of them. There are still wild cats around and people say they are descendants of her cats.

Memorial Flowers
Note cat on right top step

Kathi: Do you think she is one of the ghosts?

Rick: No. The ghosts go 'way back. The man who lived here directly before she did is not involved, either.

Janice: He lives in Colorado Spring. He doesn't say much about the ghosts.

Rick: Most of the things have happened just recently...since we came. Though the woman, I'll call her Ann, told several friends of an experience she had while living here. It seems she had been awakened by music and laughter and a lot of foot stomping. She peered over the banister. There was no one downstairs. No music. No voices. Yet the furniture had been moved out of the parlor and the carpet rolled up, evidence that a happy group of people had been dancing. Perturbed but weary, Ann decided to go back to bed and rearrange the furniture later. To her great surprise the next morning, the carpet was down, chairs and sofa were back in the parlor. Then she saw these little impressions in the carpet, proof that the furniture *had* been moved and had not been put back exactly as it had been.

Janice: A friend I had not seen in years came to visit us. She asked me to tell her about our ghosts. I said it was really nothing...some people said they heard people walking and that kind of thing. She said, "Oh, Janice, that really gives me chills! I lay there for an hour last night thinking I heard people walking in the hall."

Rick: My uncle was here, one time. He slept downstairs. The next day, he was quite irate. He wanted to know what I was doing after he had gone to bed. He said, "You were walking on those hardwood floors upstairs. Sounded

17

like you had combat boots on." I argued that I had not been upstairs, but he wouldn't believe me. Finally I told him to go upstairs. I knew he would see that all the floors are now carpeted. He came back down for breakfast but wouldn't say a word. I said, "You got something to say, Uncle?" He just grunted, "I don't want to talk about it."

Janice: Many of the guests say they hear footsteps.

Rick: We don't talk about ghosts before bedtime. We don't want guests to get ideas. Guests are usually assembled around the table while I prepare breakfast. I greet them with, "I hope you all had a pleasant rest. And I trust our permanent guests did not interrupt your sleep. If nobody reacts, I let it drop. But more often than not there will be some red faces or a wife will nudge her husband. Then I'll know something happened. We talk about it. Everyone seems excited and feels they were entertained beyond their expectations.

Kathi: What types of things happen to them? Other than footsteps and knocking?

Rick: Voices from the next room. Which can not be living people. The bedroom walls have all been sound proofed, so guests will have quiet and privacy. Sometimes we have to take a guest upstairs and prove that one can not hear another in the next room, even when they are talking quite loudly.

Janice: Sometimes they hear knocking on the door. But no one is there.

Rick: One lady was quite angry. She claimed she had not slept a wink. She asked why we never answered our phone. There are no phones in the rooms; only the one down here. I told her I had not heard it ring. She only grew more upset. I assured her I would check with the phone company, immediately. For a moment, I really thought something was wrong with the phone. I went into the office to get her a gift certificate to placate her. Then I thought of the caller ID system we had installed. It registers every call, whether or not the phone is answered. I showed her how it worked. She was finally convinced there were no calls during the night. No earthly ones, at least.

Janice: There was a woman here once who was a kind of psychic, I guess. She said someone had died in the house or on the property. She couldn't elaborate. She saw those little baby shoes in the cabinet there. She asked if we had found those in the house, which we had. She held them in her hand for a moment. Then she said a little crippled girl had worn them. That gave me goosebumps.

Rick: Chip Page once brought some men from the Springs. They were really strange. They would not go upstairs at all. One of them stood at the bottom of the steps, just dying to go up, but he wouldn't. Another one wandered toward the back of the house, where the old kitchen used to be. Suddenly he backed off, shook his head and shrugged his shoulders. He started for the front door. "Are you all right?" I asked him. "Yeah, sure," he mumbled. But he was white as a sheet. "Something frightened you around that old kitchen," I said. Finally he said, "Have you dug up any bodies back there, yet? There's something buried there." I told him we hadn't found any bodies, but there was an old cistern buried there.

"I know," he said, "I saw that, too." I told him it was under the floor, that he could not possibly see it." He repeated, firmly, "I saw it."

Janice: And then there was that other guy...

Rick: Yeah. He was walking up and down the street looking at the house, as if he didn't know which house he was looking for. We didn't have any numbers up, yet. I talked to him and he asked if he could come in the house.

Janice: I was standing in the doorway. I didn't want him to come in. I am not uncomfortable around anyone but he scared me. I didn't want him in this house. He kept talking about the house. Very weird. I felt he had been here before.

Rick: Yet, he didn't even know which house he was looking for. I blocked the door, because I could see Janice did not want him in. I asked him questions and he gave the right answers. Not answers I expected a stranger to give, but the *right* answers. He knew all about this house! I told him about the man who was afraid of the old kitchen and how he had seen the old cistern beneath the floor. "Yes," the stranger replied, "I see it, too." "You can't see it from here," I said. "It's in the back of the house, under the floor." "I'll show you," he said and pushed past me. He walked directly to the old kitchen and drew a circle with his foot. I knew he was 100% percent right. That ring was right dab on top of the cistern. Yet he still claimed he had never been in the house.

Janice: Later, he came back to stay with us. He was writing a book about the unusual things that had happened in his life.

Rick: I told him it really bothered us that he could

know about the cistern. He just said he could see things like that sometimes.

Janice: He seemed like a nice enough guy, but he wouldn't talk much. He sure had us mystified. We had put him in the Womack room. He was there a few days. Then he told us he would like to change rooms. He said nothing happened in his room, but that there were apparitions in the Goodman room. So we moved him and he seemed much happier.

Rick: One morning he came downstairs looking odd. "Well," he announced, "that was a weird night." "What's the matter?" I asked. He said he had left his laptop computer open, but it was off...unplugged in fact. Nevertheless when he woke up, he found a message on the screen. But he wouldn't tell us what.

Janice: He would never say what he was writing. Or what, if anything, he was experiencing in the way of ghosts. I asked him several times why he had come to Cripple Creek, but he wouldn't answer. Finally one day, I asked him if he believed he had been here in another life. Then he got rather talkative. "I don't know," he said, "Perhaps I was. I read a book one time. In it was a poem:

> A crooked little house
> On a crooked little street
> In a crooked little town
> Called Cripple Creek.

And I knew I had to find that little house."

Victor Hotel

THE VICTOR HOTEL

What people remember most about the Victor Hotel is the elevator. And a splendid thing it is. Dated 1900, it is still the talk of the District. Wrought iron strips twist to the top, ending in a lofty "birdcage" dome of graceful swirls and curves. It is truly a work of art.

The four-story brick exterior has the look of a business building. Typical of that era, there are decorative touches. The top floor windows are arched, echoing the arched entryway.

The Woods brothers, who platted the town, built the Hotel Victor in the mid-1890's. That hotel was a luxurious Victorian inn, drawing the curious wealthy to the "City of Mines" hidden away in the Rocky Mountains. The prosperous Hotel Victor hosted high-society parties as well as many civic and political events. The town of Victor was a mere five years old, with a population of 18,000 when fire swept through in 1899. The Hotel Victor was only one of hundreds of building consumed by the fast moving inferno.

Victor was booming. Millions of dollars in gold ore poured out of the mines. Stock exchanges and banks had been destroyed and needed to be rebuilt. The Woods brothers changed their focus. They would erect a solid

building to house the Woods Brothers Investment Company and the First National Bank. Upstairs would be simple rooms for businessmen and mine workers. Someone else could cater to the carriage trade.

We interviewed the manager and two employees to learn about the Victor Hotel and its ghostly inhabitants. Mike Randolph, current hotel manager, is a relative newcomer to the Cripple Creek District. He showed us numerous photographs of days gone by, but referred us to Joe Fitzgerald for more information.

Kathi: Were you a part of the construction crew when the hotel was renovated?

Joe: No, but I was around. I've always loved the hotel because of its history. It was good to see it come back to life, after standing empty for so long.

Kathi: When did it open as the current Victor Hotel?

Joe: About 1992. It took a long time to restore it. The city wanted it listed on the National Register of Historic Places, so the contractors had to work carefully. They retained as much of the original material as they could. Actually, the building had been built soundly. Very little work was needed on either the foundation or the brick walls. Most of the flooring and the woodwork only had to be refinished, not replaced. They added bathrooms to the upstairs rooms, but many of the old sinks in the bedrooms were saved. A few of the new bathrooms have old claw-foot tubs, as well. Steam radiators, light fixtures, even doorknobs and hinges are the ones in the building since 1900.

WEIGHT OF CAGE ▓▓▓ LBS. 1900 CAPACITY ▓▓▓ LBS.

OTIS ELEVATOR
COMPANY

NEW YORK   CHICAGO

Kathi: The Victorian furnishings of today's lobby are not typical of the original hotel?

Joe: Typical Victorian, of course. But not of this building. The first floor was a bank. But, the bank was quite prestigious. There may have been a small lounge for patrons. It would have been furnished similarly. A lot of money changed hands in those early days and competition between financial houses was understandably high. The Woods brothers knew their bank needed to look prosperous, as well as dependable, to draw the clientele they desired. The wide windows and polished woodwork helped do that. The safe you see in the lobby is actually only the faceplate of the original safe. People couldn't help but believe their deposits were secure in a safe as huge as that! Of course, the biggest draw was the elevator. It was the first elevator in the District. Birdcage elevators were very popular, but usually found only in more exclusive hotels. I'm sure it gave the investors the idea that Victor was a city to reckon with. Victor citizens were proud of that elevator and they still are.

Kathi: So, in it's beginning days, the building contained a bank on the first floor, hotel in the upper three?

Joe: Yes, although it changed functions as the needs of Victor changed. They say there was once a bar on the mezzanine. The second floor was converted to offices for lawyers and mine owners early in the century. At one time there was a small hospital on the top floor. Lowell Thomas' father was one of the physicians that served that hospital. Of course, as gold prices

27

fell and mining declined a great variety of tenants took over, each a little shakier, financially, until in the 80's the building was abandoned.

Kathi: What can you tell me of paranormal events that take place here?

Joe: The only thing I, personally, have seen is the elevator. It activates itself, going up and down with no one near it. It is inspected and maintained, as required by law, on a periodic basis. The inspectors assure us it is in perfect working condition, with no malfunctions. The mechanics claim there is no possible way it can operate itself. Still, I have often been the only person in the hotel and have heard that elevator start and watched it rise and then descend. I agree it cannot happen, but it does.

Kathi: How do you explain that?

Joe: No one can explain it, but it is undoubtedly tied in with Eddie.

Kathi: Tell me about Eddie.

Joe: Apparently he lived in the hotel in the early part of the century. His room was number 301. In piecing together all the stories told, Eddie was probably a miner or a mine supervisor. No one remembers his last name or very much about him. He might never have come to public attention except that he accidentally fell down the elevator shaft and killed himself. He was laid out in the room he had rented. Room 301.

Kathi: And he is still here?

Joe: For whatever reason, he is still here. Still walking back and forth to the communal bathroom or to chat with other tenants. Guests come to the front desk and tell me they have

Room 301

Eddie's Room

	been awakened by footsteps outside their door. But when they look into the hall no one is there.
Kathi:	Are they frightened?
Joe:	Curious more than anything else. Everyone seems to have a different explanation of what they heard...an old building creaking...other guests going to their rooms...the old radiators...even the wind. I don't think any of them really believed it was a ghost. But a lot of people think the possibility of a ghost outside their hotel door is fascinating – something to tell the folks back home.
Kathi:	Do you tell them about Eddie?
Joe:	It depends on the person. Some get very interested. Then I'll talk about Eddie.
Kathi:	Do you believe Eddie is walking around on the third floor?
Joe:	I have never seen him. Or heard him. But, sure, I can believe Eddie is here. I once owned a Victorian house in Galveston. There was a ghost in there. His name was Henry. He had been a wealthy merchant and he built the house himself. Then he was killed in that house during a hurricane. I'm not sure just how it happened, because the house was not destroyed by the storm. But it was his home and he refused to leave it. I heard him a lot, walking around, talking to someone. I saw him a couple of times. I did not believe in ghosts until then. But, I do now. For sure! Something other than a living being starts that elevator. It goes to the third floor, every time. It pauses, opens, and then closes and descends. You can stand anywhere in the lobby and hear all those sounds. I'm convinced it is poor old Eddie.

Kathi: Why do you suppose he is a ghost? Why is he still here?

Joe: I'd be pretty smart if I knew that, wouldn't I? I figure Eddie was a hard working man. Got up at dawn to go to work, opened the elevator door, probably half asleep, and stepped in. Except the elevator was not there. Eddie fell to the bottom. His body was broken to bits, but his mind, or his soul or something couldn't take that all in. He doesn't know he no longer has a body. He carries on with what he has always known. He goes to work and comes back home to his room. Room 301. That's the only way I can think of it.

Joe took us up to room 301. It is on the front corner of the hotel, quite near the elevator. Two walls are brick, matching the bricks of the exterior, with brick arches over windows overlooking the mountains. Lace curtains flutter in the breeze. A steam radiator provides heat – one of original radiators. A light fixture with etched glass shade graces the wall above an antique sink. The doorknob is a round, white glass globe. The room is simply furnished with an iron bed, small table and chair. Eddie's room has not changed all that much since he lived there decades ago.

Downstairs again, we talked to Vern Evans, also an employee of the hotel. Vern was born and raised in Victor and has vivid memories of the building.

Vern: Did they tell you there was a mine under the bank in the old days?

Kathi: No. That must have been handy for the depositor.

Vern: Yeah. Well, there's probably an old mine under every building in this town. It's truly a

Victor Hotel - 1900

----

wonder we haven't all fallen in!

Kathi: Did you play in mines when you were small?

Vern: Only when there was no one around. That's the first thing you learn when you grow up in a mining town...stay away from holes in the ground!

Kathi: What do you remember about this building?

Vern: The building was deserted when I was a kid. We used to break into it and wander around. We knew there had been dead bodies on the fourth floor, when the hospital was there. As you know, the ground is frozen solid here from October to June. Back then, they had no heavy equipment to dig graves. So the bodies were stored up there until summer. That made it a special, spooky place for kids to play. We used to lure a new kid up there, tie him to the doorknob and run away. Soon found out if he was a sissy!

Kathi:	There have been rumors of ghosts of doctors. And patients with no arms or legs. Even one without a head.
Vern:	Probably told by one of those kids we tormented! I've not known anyone who has seen such ghosts.
Kathi:	So Eddie is your only ghost?
Vern:	As far as I know. Again, I have not encountered him.
Kathi:	He only appears in room 301?
Vern:	Mostly. One man said he was standing at the foot of his bed, staring at him.
Kathi:	Had this man heard Eddie's story before seeing him?
Vern:	No. But he claimed he saw him. Said he was wearing a plaid shirt. Said he looked like a miner to him.
Kathi:	Did he know Eddie's name?
Vern:	Didn't say so.
Kathi:	What have other guests seen?
Vern:	Nothing. Maybe a misty form of some kind, in the hall, after they heard footsteps. There was one lady who followed a man into the elevator, but when she got in, the man had disappeared. So she said, anyway.
Kathi:	Have you seen the elevator go up and down when no one was in it?
Vern:	Oh yes. It happens quite often. Mostly in the middle of the night or very early in the morning. I'll be sitting at the front desk and hear it. I don't even bother to get up and check it out anymore.
Kathi:	Do you believe in ghosts?
Vern:	Oh, I don't know. It's hard to know what goes on in people's minds...what they think they see or hear, but only dreamed. What might be

the influence of too much liquor…or troubles no one knows about.

I, myself, have never experienced anything. But if old Eddie is still here, taking the elevator up to his room and expecting to find his bed empty, well… it's all right with me. I don't bother him and he don't bother me.

We left the Victor Hotel, its quiet dignity, its splendid turn of the century elegance showing through. At the door I turned again toward the birdcage elevator. It stood still. I guess it was too early for Eddie to come home from the mines.

St. Nicholas Hospital

CRIPPLE CREEK, COLORADO

Conducted by the Sisters of Mercy

Rules and Regulations

Admission of Patients

The Hospital is open to receive patients at all hours of the day or night irrespective of creed or nationality.

Regulations for Visitors.

Visits of relatives or friends are allowed daily from 9:30 to 11 a. m., 2 to 4, and 7 to 8:15 p. m. No night visits will be permitted except in cases of extreme urgency. Visitors from a distance must take accommodations outside the Hospital.

Meals are not served to relatives or friends of patients, neither are such relatives or friends allowed to remain with patients over night unless requested by the Sister in charge. In order to avoid noise and disturbance children will not be admitted to visit unless accompanied by parents or guardians.

VISITING DAYS—Strangers wishing to visit the Hospital will be admitted every day from 2 to 4 p. m.

DOORS CLOSE AT 9:30 P. M.

Rules for Patients

Hotel St. Nicholas

It's a comfort, on a cold winter night, to look across town to the lighted cross atop the St. Nicholas. For more than one hundred years, it has been a beacon of hope and faith to all who view it.

It all began when Sister Mary Baptist boarded the stage in Denver, carpetbag in hand. The bone-crushing journey up Ute Pass to Cripple Creek in 1893 was long and perilous, but her mission was worthy. She had been called to open a hospital.

The Superior of the Sisters of Mercy of Colorado found conditions in the camp deplorable. Cripple Creek

37

boasted a population of 4,000 (soon to swell to 20,000), yet less than 200 had what could be deemed adequate housing. Tents and tiny wooden shacks tumbled over each other down the hillsides. They gave almost no protection against frigid winds nor the constant summer thunderstorms. Exposure to such severe high altitude weather took its toll.

Food was scarce and expensive. Fresh fruits and vegetables were a rarity. Most children had yet to see their first orange or string bean. Bodies that needed vitamins and calcium to stave off rampant disease, received little from the steady diet of salt pork and beans.

Sanitation was non-existent. Clean drinking water became impossible to find.

Babies and young children lie sick and dying. Many mothers were not much better. Miners were injured daily in the hundreds of mines surrounding the town. Disputes in Bennett Avenue saloons often ended in knife fights and gun battles.

If ever a town needed a hospital, it was Cripple Creek, Colorado.

Sister Mary Baptist called other Sisters to help. They placed beds in a large house on East Eaton Avenue and attended all who sought help. Then Sister Mary Baptist set about to build a real hospital. She solicited the Denver Mission, friends in Colorado Springs, local Lodges, Cripple Creek merchants, miners, saloon keepers and shady ladies on Myers Avenue. When money ran low she renewed her fund raising efforts and squeezed out a little more wherever she could. Brick by brick the building rose three stories high. After four years and a total cost of $12,000 the magnificent hospital was finished. It boasted steam heat, electric lights, hot and cold water and surgical facilities. Prominent men of Cripple Creek took it upon themselves to provide needed medical equipment and to furnish patients' rooms. A. E. Carlton, Oscar Lampman, W. T. Booth and N. O. Johnson are a few of the donors recorded.

St. Nicholas Hospital was named in honor of Bishop Nicholas Matz who dedicated the hospital on the afternoon of May 15, 1898. Within minutes the first patient was admitted. Elijah Ayers had fallen down the shaft of the Specimen mine.

In 1902 an addition was made to the hospital to serve as living quarters for the Sisters.

St. Nicholas Hospital welcomed new babies. They treated frostbite and broken bones. They cared for hundreds during sieges of cholera and influenza. During the 1903-1904 strike between miners and mine owners, men were carried to the hospital on the hill every day, mutilated by clubs, guns and dynamite explosions. The sisters patched them up the best they could. When all hope was gone, they sent a kitchen boy across the street to fetch the Priest from St. Peters Catholic Church to say the last rites.

In the decades following the strike, Cripple Creek's fortunes began to decline. Mines closed and people moved on. St. Nicholas struggled. In 1925, it was forced to close. Dr. W. Hassenplug bought the hospital. It then became known as The Cripple Creek Hospital. Later Dr. Hassenplug turned it over to Dr. A. C. Denman, a man remembered fondly in Cripple Creek, today.

The hospital closed its doors for the last time in the mid-seventies. Then it stood empty for twenty years.

The old brick building fascinated friends Noel and Denise Perran and Kurt and Susan Adelbush. In April, 1995, after months of inspections and investigations, they purchased the building. Their goal was a hotel reflecting the elegance of earlier Cripple Creek hotels. While Noel and Kurt repaired and replaced, hammered and plumbed and painted, Susan and Denise gathered carpets, drapes, furniture and accessories in a hearty blend of Victorian and Country decors. The result is breath taking. Vivid colors flow throughout the hallways. Accents of ruffles and lace

The Hotel St. Nicholas
HISTORIC MOUNTAIN INN

adorn every bedroom. Hotel St. Nicholas offers the warmth of 1898 plus all the comforts of today. Guests enjoy breakfast in the bright dining room. Evenings bring music and fun in the Boiler Room Tavern on the lower floor. The focal point of this popular pub is the faceplate of the original 1898 boiler that heated the building.

I interviewed the Adelbushes and the Perrans, as well as Amy Willard, a long time employee in the Tavern. For our first meeting, I took along a tape recorder. Before leaving home, I checked batteries and made sure everything was in working order. Just before I got out of the car, I turned it on again, satisfied it was fine.

As we sat down to talk, I turned on the recorder. It did not record. I turned it on and off and on and off, checked the battery again, tapped it on the table. Nothing worked. The recorder refused to cooperate. Someone said, "The ghosts don't want to be talked about!" and we all laughed. I did the interview with no tape recorder and few notes; I became so fascinated with their stories I could only watch their animated faces and listen.

Susan started us off:

Susan: We began to hear tales of ghosts soon after we bought the building.
Denise: But none of us had ever seen a ghost, so we discounted the stories. We were too busy to think about ghosts. Anyway, big empty buildings are always scary to me.
Susan: Yes. You hear noises, floor creakings and such, and you are not sure where they come from.
Denise: I'm much more concerned that it may be a live stranger who is not supposed to be here than I am that it may be a ghost.

41

Susan: There are so many people around, now that we have opened, that you soon get used to footsteps and voices.

Denise: I'm not sure, even now, that I believe in ghosts. Still... a lot of people do.

Kurt: I have never felt anything uncomfortable in this building. Even when I was here alone I felt only a welcoming feeling.

Susan: Yes. It's not a scary place. Not anymore. We've talked about it. Even if there are ghosts, we feel they must want us here. At least they have not chased us away!

Noel: I must admit, I felt differently at first. I did most of the inspections. I crawled up in the attic, into all the little nooks and crannies, and under the building. There used to be a tunnel under the street to the church. Old-timers say the nuns used it in the foul weather. They were braver than I. To me it was spooky!

Kathi: Did you go through the tunnel?

Noel: No. We found the beginning of it, but it was in such bad condition we did not try to go all the way. We cemented it up.

Kathi: Could you tell where it came out at the church?

Noel: No. Nobody seems to know. They offered to let us poke around, but we had too much else to do, so we gave that up. There used to be another building on the south of the church – a small chapel, someone said. Probably that was the end of the tunnel. At any rate, this building was scary while I was exploring all those dark, dank places.

Kathi: Did you see or hear anything that might have been ghosts?

Noel: No. I just had those creepy-crawlies anyone would have in such places.

42

Kurt: At one time, when the building was unoccupied, miners and penniless travelers were allowed to sleep here. Several of them came back while we were working on the building. The stories they told would literally curl your hair.

Denise: You have to wonder how much they made up. Or what part too much to drink had to do with what they said.

Noel: Well, it's not surprising, when you think back over the years and all that happened here, that there are ghosts.

Kathi: Tell me some of your experiences.

Susan: I have not seen anything...well maybe a movement, a shadow out of the corner of my eye. I always rationalized it was my wild imagination or something perfectly natural. But....

Denise: I sometimes feel strange in the upstairs hall. There is a picture there. It's a sweet child. A young girl. But, I feel she is watching me. I know several artists are talented enough to paint so that the subject's eyes seem to follow you. That's all that picture is. I know that. Still, I feel funny. Not frightened, really, but very strange. Amy is more sensitive than any of us.

Kathi: You've been very quiet, Amy. What can you tell me?

Amy: Plenty! I tend bar in the Boiler Room Tavern. One night a bottle of Crown Royal Special Reserve exploded. No one was near it. It just exploded. A regular customer was sitting right there on a barstool. He thought someone might have shot through the window, so he went outside and looked around. There was no one

Girl with "watching" eyes

there, nor any indication that anyone had been there. It was one of those blustery, cold snowy nights. Not the kind of night someone would willingly choose to fool around outside. There was no bullet hole in the window. There was nothing that might explain the bottle breaking. It just broke.

Kurt: I tried to reason that it was the altitude. Pressure builds up in packages when they are transported to ten thousand feet. Everything you open emits a burst of compressed air.

Amy: Except that the bottle had already been opened. So what made it explode?

Noel: We could never explain that.

Amy: My impressions began after I had worked in the bar only a few nights. I felt someone standing beside me. Like a man flirting with me. He ruffled my hair. Sometimes he would touch my clothing. Just barely. But there was no one behind the bar, where I was. They were all sitting at the tables, or the barstools. So I thought of a ghost. I know a man very much into paranormal stuff. We had an interesting talk about it. He agreed it was probably a ghost. He said not to be upset about it. "No one has ever been killed by a ghost," he told me.

Kathi: So you stopped being afraid?

Amy: I was not afraid, anyway. Just a little antsy about what might happen next. Then last Halloween one of the local newspapers brought in several psychics for their annual ghost hunt. One of them sensed this guy, too. She said it was not a man, but a little boy, one of the orphans the nuns had taken in. She said the nuns would feed and take care of them until

45

someone came to get them. They would give them chores to do. She asked what this room was before it was remodeled. I told her it was the laundry room, and that the kitchen was nearby. "So this is the section of the building he knows best. He just wants you to know he is here."

Noel: Knowing he is a little boy explained some other things. He must be the one who plays with the little frog we keep on the cash register. Sometimes the frog appears on the bar, someone's chair or back among the bottles. Customers could be responsible for part of it, I suppose, but they could not put the frog on the back bar unless they threw it.

Amy: We call the little boy, Petey. He steals my cigarettes. I say, give them back, Petey. Then I turn around and there they are. He is quite attached to me. I feel him around me all the time. He even calls me by name.

Kathi: Oh! Does he speak to anyone else?

Amy: No. It's like he is teasing me, bragging that he knows who I am. He's kinda mischievous, but I think it's because he's lonesome.

Kathi: Does anyone else know he is there?

Amy: Sometimes. I've seen people look around them, very oddly. When I ask if anything is wrong they laugh and say, no. One man said he knew it was silly but he felt like someone was watching him. It was Petey, of course. I think Petey would like it if more people recognized him.

Susan: A really odd thing happened before we opened the hotel. There was this awful smell around the back staircase.

Stinky's Staircase

Denise: Yes! It was a smell that none of us could recognize. It wasn't quite like a dead animal, or mold, or sewage...

Kurt: But that's what we decided it must be. Sewage. We had the plumbers here several times. They were adamant it was not a sewage problem. In fact, they declared they could smell nothing at all.

Amy: That was one of the strange things about it. It was not consistent. Sometimes it would drive you out of the hall; other times you could not smell anything.

Susan: It was so embarrassing. We planned to open in a few days and we knew no one would stay once they smelled that hallway.

Denise: Then one day I was vacuuming the carpet near the stairs. Chip Page, our local historian and ghost storyteller was leading a group of tourists through the hotel. As they came down the stairs he told them one of the stories we had heard several times. People have reported seeing a man walking down the stairs. They had heard boots stomping on the stairs, even though the steps are carpeted, now. They can see him move from step to step. Then they realized there was no upper body! Only legs encased in miner's boots. Then, Chip told the tourist group that people called this ghost "Stinky" because he had a horrible odor!

Susan: You should have seen her face when she ran in here to tell me about it!

Denise: You should have seen *her* face when she heard about it!

Kathi: Have any of you seen Stinky?

Noel: No.

Kathi: Have you smelled him again?

Denise: No. Once in a while I'll see a guest walk down the steps and wrinkle their nose like they smell something peculiar.

Amy: I encountered him a few weeks ago. I was in the Tavern alone. I was just opening up. I was in a rush because I was expecting a group of special guests. All of a sudden I smelled Stinky. Once you have smelled him, you never mistake that smell! I said aloud, "Oh Stinky! Not now!" And he went away.

Kathi: Is this stairway you speak of the one I came by when I came in from the parking lot?

Noel: No, it's back here. You haven't seen all of the building, have you? Let's take a tour.

Noel led us past the tavern door to a back hall, which was roped off with a velvet rope. An outside door stood at the end of the hall. Burgundy colored carpeting led to the second level. The banister had been newly refinished. Noel first went past the stairs and opened doors to a couple of rooms.

Noel: This is still unfinished. This room catches all the surplus stuff, at the moment. Including the old operating table. I'm not sure what we are going to do with it.

Susan: We seldom use the outside door. Since this was part of the nuns living quarters, perhaps they used it to walk in the garden or go over to the church.

Amy: Sometimes people get lost if there is no one at the front desk when they come in. I try to watch for them as they go past the tavern door. But there is one lady I have not caught. She looks as real as anyone does, but she is of another time. She wears a long skirt and white blouse, like thousands of ladies you have seen in pictures taken at the turn of the century. And she has her hair up in a bun. She walks from the front hall back here. She doesn't turn if I call her. And when I rush to the hall, she is gone.

Kathi: She is not dressed as a nun?

Amy: No. I have seen her several times, but I have no idea who she might be.

Noel: These upstairs floors were made of Long Pine, brought in from Missouri or Kentucky. Colorado pine is not as hard and would not have lasted so long. The woodwork is all original, as well. These deep scars were made when the gurneys scrapped against the doorways.

Susan: Notice the heavy wire screen in the glass of the windows in this room.

Noel: This room is directly above the Tavern. One night a woman came in, ordered a drink. She drank it rather rapidly, looking around in a strange manner. Then she got up and wandered around the hotel a bit and left! Another guest told me the woman had said she couldn't stay because of the room above her. This room.

Kathi: What was this room? Why was she so frightened?

Noel: She may have sensed more than we have. The wire in the window glass leads us to believe this is where violent or mental cases were held.

Kathi: It is so lovely, now, with your floral décor. One would never guess it was any thing but a comfortable hotel room.

Denise: Here is another bedroom. All of them have lots of light. We did not have to add windows.

The nuns must have liked sunlight, too.

Kurt: There is a solarium here on the sunny side of the building. It was the nursery. Some of the babies had jaundice. They put them here in the sun to heal them.

Susan: Many of our guests have reported they heard a baby cry in here.

Noel: Which reminds me of another story. A friend and I were sitting here one morning; it is such a pleasant room. We were expecting his wife and little girl. We heard movement in the hall and a small child's fussing. My friend got up to go meet them. But there was no one there. His wife had not yet arrived. The baby we heard was obviously not his child.

Kurt: There is only one bedroom, now, without its own bath. This bathroom off the hall, is for their use. The sink and the claw foot tub are both original. As is the wall tile. We saved as many tubs and sinks as we could. We did replace all the toilets. I suspect they had been replaced several times anyway. This bathroom evidently was not used very much. It had one of those old fashioned toilets with the oak tank on top.

Denise: And a chain pull!

Susan: We would have loved to keep it. But it made so much noise when you flushed it we were afraid it would wake all the guests.

Kurt: Oh, it gurgled and whined...

Amy: And gasped and howled!

Kurt: So we took it out.

Amy: But we still hear it flush! Especially at night.

Denise: It is a very distinctive sound. Not at all like any of the other toilets. It is very disconcerting to hear a toilet flush, when you know that toilet is not even in the building.

Susan: This is the old dumb-waiter where meals were brought up and dishes sent back to the kitchen.

Noel: This corner room is number eleven. Once a guest met me in the hall and said, "Room eleven was the surgery, wasn't it?" I did not know that. So she explained. "It has a slight ramp into the room, so the gurney did not have to go over a threshold. It is a small room. There are windows on two sides, but the bottom parts of the windows are opaque so you can not see in from the outside. And you added heat, didn't you?" she went on, "when it was used as an operating room, it had no heat. This small cabinet or closet just outside the door was used for dressings, drugs and other things that needed to be handy, but not in the room where they might be contaminated by a patient." I was dumbfounded and asked her when she had been in the hospital. She laughed. She said she was from Indianapolis and had never been in Colorado before. Also, she knew very little about hospitals, old or new. "It is simply that I see things, sometimes," she said. I took her down to the room we just left, with the wire windows and asked her what she thought about that. She agreed the wire was for the safety of violent and mentally ill patients. "The protective wire was put in," she said, "after a man jumped out of the window. He was out of his head with fever." I asked if he died. She said she didn't know, but the fever would have killed him anyway.

Kathi: What a story! Do you get many guests like that?

Susan: No, but we have had a few. Some actually ask when they check in, if we have ghosts and where they might find them.
Kathi: And do they find them?
Susan: I don't think so. Ghosts don't seem to perform when you want them to.
Noel: We have seen the second and third floors. These steps lead to the attic. They are very narrow and we don't allow guests up here. The attic, as you can see, runs the length of the building. It too, has windows at each end for light.
Kathi: I see the train and other toys. Do your children play here?
Noel: Yes, it makes a great playroom. In the old days it was the nuns dormitory. Then they added the east wing so they could have their own bedrooms and be closer to the patients.
Kurt: This is the cupola, where the cross is.
Kathi: Oh, it's neat to see it from this angle. Do you know when it was installed?
Kurt: I suspect at the very beginning, when the building was built. The Church would have wanted it in place immediately.
Kathi: One hundred years ago. Amazing!
Susan: We came up the back way. Now we will go down the front way.
Kathi: It's nice that you leave the guestroom doors open.
Susan: Yes. Guests like to peek in the other rooms. It seems cozier than a hallway of closed doors. We only close the doors after the rooms are occupied. We are fully booked tonight, but most guests have not yet checked in.
Noel: This is the picture that scares Denise.
Denise: It doesn't scare me. It just makes me very

uncomfortable.

Susan: Her eyes do follow you. But isn't she sweet!

Kurt: This grandfather clock belonged to my family. We have tinkered and tinkered with it, but we can not make it keep time. It has only chimed once since we brought it here.

Susan: Yes. We had a lovely wedding here one afternoon. Just as the minister pronounced the couple man and wife, the clock chimed. We were all shocked, but agreed it was a good omen.

Noel: Let's go back to the Boiler room and have a cold drink. But first, I'll show you the kitchen area. You can see there is equipment enough to feed a couple of armies. We only use it for preparing a light breakfast for our guests and snacks for our pub patrons.

Susan: And ourselves.

Noel: Yeah. As you can imagine, we all spend a great deal of time here. Underneath this door in the floor is the wine cellar.

Kathi: A wine cellar in a hospital?

Noel: Well, it was a Catholic hospital, after all; sacramental wine, you know. This is the boiler room. We still use steam heat to heat the entire building. Except now we use natural gas instead of coal.

Amy: Wait 'til you see this room. It's cold and damp.

Kathi: And a perfect place to keep your beer and liquor, I see. What was it originally? A root cellar?

Noel: Not exactly. It was the morgue! Come on in the pub and sit down.

Kathi: If this is the Boiler Room Tavern and that was the boiler room in there, what was this room?

Grandfather Clock

Noel: See where the floor changes from wood to cement? The cement floor, from here to the back of the bar, was the laundry room. There is a big drain back there. We did not have to put in any plumbing – it was already here.

Amy: Someone told us half of the seating area of the Tavern was the X-ray room, the other half an examining room.

Kathi: It must have been fun, discovering where everything was in Sister Mary Baptist's day. One can well imagine what a busy place it was, people moving around, doing all sorts of chores, helping people get well. I wonder how many patients were here? Thousands, I suppose. And hundreds of nuns, over the years, and other helpers.

Noel: Some of which, apparently, are still here.

Kathi: Apparently! Do people come to stay here, knowing the hotel is haunted?

Susan: Oh yes! So many have heard about us, from all over the world.

Denise: Others don't know about the ghosts when they come, but often have some sort of experience while here.

Kathi: Tell me some of their stories.

Susan: One woman checked in, unpacked and was back down stairs within an hour. She said she could not stay. That there were too many people in her room.

Noel: Most people don't react that way, however. Some of them are just puzzled. They have no idea they have seen a ghost. Many are excited to be a part of the action. Nobody has fled in terror. One woman swore we were showing "The Sound of Music" in the attic. She heard the nuns singing.

Lobby – Hotel Saint Nicholas

Denise: A man saw a nun's face in his mirror. When he turned around, of course, no one was there.

Noel: My brother came to stay with us one night. He pooh-poohed all our tales of spirits. He was tired and wanted a quiet room off to itself, so I put him in the corner room on the top floor.

The next morning when he came down, he was angry with me. He asked why I rented the next room to a family with kids. He claimed the kids were running up and down the hall, bouncing a ball in the middle of the night. I asked if he had told them to be quiet. He said, no he was too tired to get up. And, too mad. Said he might have killed the little brats. I told him if he had looked out into the hallway, he

57

would not have seen anyone. I swore to him that he was the only guest on that side of the floor. He finally realized I meant what I said and he became a firm believer in ghosts!

Kathi: You must all be firm believers by now!

Denise: Not really. It's pretty hard to accept.

Amy: I don't find it hard at all. There is no other way to explain what I have seen and heard.

Susan: And felt. And *smelled*!

Kurt: I would like to believe in ghosts. I really would. Still, I don't think I do. But, as Amy says, there are things that go on in this place that simply cannot be explained. Such as...

Susan: The dog!

Kurt: Yes. I am with the Colorado Springs police force, the canine corp. I train attack dogs. The dog I currently have, I raised from a pup. He has received all his training from me. He is with me all the time. He is a great dog.

Susan: That's right. The kids all love him. He is so gentle with them. He protects them, too.

Kurt: But, when need be, he can be a killer. To get on with my story: Rex is always with me. So he is familiar with this building, familiar with Noel and his family. One night I was in the Boiler Room Tavern, cleaning up. I was the only one in the building. Rex was lying in the doorway, sleeping. I heard the outside door open and someone come in. I was expecting Noel and thought nothing of it. When Noel was within a few feet of the tavern door, Rex jumped up and instantly went into an attack mode. My first thought was that he was going to attack Noel. I yelled at Rex to stop. But he raced past Noel and up the stairs. Then I knew he was onto something. "Come on, Noel,"

I yelled, "you gotta see this." We chased the dog up three flights of stairs. By the time he reached the third floor we were about half a flight behind him. We got to the landing and there was the dog, lying in front of a closed door, calm as if nothing had happened.

Kathi: Now wait a minute. Start from the beginning and tell me what really happened. The dog was not after Noel, right?

Kurt: No. Noel would be dead meat.

Kathi: So, was the dog protecting you?

Kurt: No. If he were protecting me, he never would have left me.

Kathi: So something was on the stairs and he was chasing it?

Kurt: Not necessarily. These dogs are trained to smell or sense things anywhere in a building or even from the outside of a building.

Kathi: So there was something upstairs he was after? Something he didn't like?

Kurt: Something that he was compelled to attack. Yes.

Kathi: And that something was in the room behind the door?

Kurt: No. If it was, Rex would be clawing the door down.

Kathi: So it just disappeared, this thing.

Kurt: The thing, whatever it was, did not disappear. Rex would still be searching for it. He would never give up until he found it.

Kathi: I'm completely confused! What happened?

Kurt: This thing, as we keep calling it, calmed down the dog. The dog was no longer compelled to attack. He was content with matters as they were.

Kathi: What do you suppose it was? This thing?

59

Kurt: Good question. Something Rex had not sensed before. Something that aroused and enraged him. Something that liked, or had liked, dogs. Something capable of making Rex feel quite relaxed with the situation.

Kathi: How could you not believe in ghosts after that incident?

Kurt: As I say, some things defy all explanation.

I said goodbye to Amy, the Perrans and the Adelbushes, thanking them all for a delightful and informative evening.

Curious, I turned on the tape recorder before starting my car. I spoke a few words, then rewound it.

My voice came back to me, loud and clear.

*****

Kathi Mac Iver and her husband consider themselves fortunate to live in the historic town of Cripple Creek, Colorado.

Kathi Mac Iver has written poetry, a Civil War documentary, non-fiction and fiction including several novels. Her books about Cripple Creek have given her great satisfaction. The percept of yesteryear abounds in this land in the sky, a constant reminder of those who built the foundation of the World's Greatest Gold Camp. Today their bones may molder in Mt. Pisgah cemetery, but their spirits forever linger in this place they called home.